Given

ROGER GARFITT

GIVEN GROUND

CARCANET

First published in 1989 by
Carcanet Press Limited
208-212 Corn Exchange Buildings
Manchester M4 3BQ UK

British Library Cataloguing in Publication Data

Garfitt, Roger
  Given ground
  I. Title
  821'.914

  ISBN 0-85635-811-8

The Publisher acknowledges financial assistance from
the Arts Council of Great Britain.

Typeset in 10pt Palatino by Bryan Williamson, Manchester
Printed in England by SRP Ltd., Exeter

for Frances

Acknowledgements

My thanks are due to the Editors of the following magazines where these poems first appeared: *Aquarius, Aspect* (Australia), *The Honest Ulsterman, Iowa Review, London Magazine, New Statesman, Outposts, Pacific Quarterly Moana, Poetry Wales, PN Review, Slightly Soiled, Stand, TLS, La Traductière* (Paris); and to the Editors of the following anthologies: *Between Comets* (poems in honour of Norman Nicholson); *First and Always* (the Great Ormond Street Children's Hospital anthology); *New Poems 1976-77* (the PEN anthology) and *New Poetry 5, 6, 7,* and *8* (the Arts Council/PEN anthologies); *1982 Anthology* (Sotheby's International Poetry Competition); 1983 Poetry Book Society Christmas Supplement; *Presences of Nature* (Carlisle Museum & Art Gallery); *Singing Brink* (the Lumb Bank anthology); and *Wall* (LYC Press). 'The Night Self' first appeared as a Mandeville Press Dragoncard. Eleven of these poems appeared as a Northern House pamphlet, *The Broken Road* (1982). I have reprinted 'Hares Boxing' from *West of Elm* (Carcanet, 1975) in order to record one small but important change of phrase. I am indebted to Terry Eagleton for pointing out the insufficiency of the original phrase.

I wish to acknowledge financial assistance from the Arts Council of Great Britain, and the provision of two Arts Council Fellowships, at the University College of North Wales and at Sunderland Polytechnic; also short-term residencies funded by Northern Arts, the South-East Wales Arts Association, and Lincolnshire and Humberside Arts.

My deepest and most particular thanks must go to John Arrowsmith and Carolina Ospina, whose home became my home during Frances' months in hospital in London, and has been a haven since. Several of these poems were brought to completion under their roof.

Contents

Buzzard Soaring

So long grounded

in himself, under such
feather weight

he seems to rise
out of a sack.

A dead poundage
re-assembles on the wings

spread into a sycamore key
turning. Earth breathes him out,

exhales him from his vantage,
to glide with the traffic between worlds,

the exploding galaxies of spores,
the seeds suspended in their shrouds.

The equality, the lightness here . . .
He feels his shadow separate

and travel the air, another
wanderer, another dust.

Below, history fires its
intricate acreage. Demesnes melt.

Towns bleed across ploughland.
Motorways grub like glaciers.

He suns. He sleepwalks on the wing
through this world and the next,

hearing the hormones hiss, hearing
the froth in his cells: *Re-enter*

the inferno. Rise again as ash.

Four Windows

One window looks over the ground
this cottage used to rent,
the thin strips across the river
they ditched and drained,
winter floodplain
where the yearlings summered:
now the plats have gone back
and the marsh climbs the hill.

One window looks over the road
to the stalls and shippons,
five sheds in a quarter acre:
haphazard joinery,
higgler's pigsties;
a carved pew-end hangs as a door,
latched with a nail; working silence,
whose uses lack their second hand.

One window looks to the hill slopes,
to the smooth sheep runs: half the year
a weather eye is all they need.
No half measures would work this land
that needs thrift and dry weather to
come together,
or dead growth and damp scorches it:
now below the contour
disuse is a slow fire.

One window looks back to my desk
– thriftless trade, whose measures
take time-and-a-half to complete.
One tune only answers
either master,
that ditch and line run clear, and sing.
I set my scale, work to this ground,
who can work it no other way.

Hares Boxing

for Nigel Wells

This way and that
goes the runaway furrow.
Nose to tail
goes the tunnel
in the grass.

Now the leader
swivels, jerks up his heels.
The trick flickers
along the rope of hares:
heels over head they go, head over heels.

It's the Saturday
after Valentine:
in Florey's Stores
the kids go
into huddles,

Oh! What did he put?
Go on, tell us! we *promise*
we won't tell.

Did she send you one?
  Did she?

Over the winter nothing has changed
but the land. The hedgerows
are in heaps for burning.
The owl's tree stands vacant
between the scars of smooth earth.

The sunlight falls on cleared spaces,
on the old lines. The hares meet
as they met before Enclosure, far out
in the drift of grasses, their fisticuffs
like tricks of the eye.

What catches the light, what the eye believes
is the rufous shoulder, the chest's white blaze:
what it sees are up on their haunches
the blaze throw its guard up, the shoulder
slide in a punch; two pugs that duel

stripped to the waist by sunlight.
And the Fancy? They emerge
from the corners of the eye, low company
from the lie of the land, with guineas
in their stare, without visible means.

The purse is all he fancies. The generations
bunch in his arm.
Toora-li-ooral go the fifes in his blood.
As tall, as straight as a thistle,
Jack Hare squares up to Dancing Jack.

Blue

Memory on a peg
behind the door:

the slip-leash a live line
through my fingers

that floats on his shoulders'
running water

or knows their stiffening
the undertow

of another presence
in the hedgebank

still rancorous with fox.
Always that shock

as the hackles rise on
a waking dream,

an ancient line stands out
in the young dog.

Slip him, and I become
the outer ear,

the iris of his eye,
ready to shout

if he conjures a fox
as he stag-leaps

and salmons the long grass.
Enter the land

within the land, a light
and shadow land

whose denizens are quick
and changing shapes,

where the pheasant's wing spreads
into dead wood,

and riddles of brown earth
in the stubble

or clods of bleached-out grass
in the furrow

soon as our backs are turned
go haring off.

Enter the light and dark
of the duel,

the dog's dive and dolphin
over the ground,

a shoulder gleam breaking
the air's surface,

a slate gleam, night closing
with each new stride,

the hare's running rings, her
lucky numbers,

noughts and figures of eight,
a breathing space

won on every turn.
Enter the dark

of that other duel
he fought, the leash

an allegiance he held,
a last life line.

Sorrow still rives me that
I let him slip.

Crows in Snow

Absences of motion, of colour.

Meteorite or moraine, black stones
half-in or half-out of the snow.

Only purpose survives

and has them belly down, black cones
of heat-absorption, solar cells

recharging in the sun

as if all has to be done again,
the ground to disclose its strata,

the minerals their millennia,

the fossil slates of Langenaltheim
split a second time, and flight feathers

print once, twice on the snow.

Gardening in Avernus

Evening in the turned earth.
A night wind foxes the grass.
Still through the late afternoon
of stone the thin scent rises
of a herb patch by the wall
and I am on a path of
that other garden where thyme
is grey bush beyond the vines,
reptile over the dry rocks.

Cicadas stir the leaf fall.
The lych-owl pronounces dusk
over shadowless cedars.
The foraging pipistrelles
enter meridian blue.
A common scent of earth is
the black ship across Ocean,
a coast of willows and mist.
Without a trench of dark blood

I have come where the tenses
elide. The past re-opens
to a nervous link through an
electronic gate, or the
Gate of Horn. Cell by single
cell an identity wakes,
as over featureless distances
the sightlines form of
particular earth and hours.

Three stanzas in memoriam W.H. Auden

Draw back the sackcloth from the windows.
Lock the revolver in the desk drawer.
Another kind of silence
is entering at the open door.
In the writing lamp's circumference,
within the ambient dust,
a concentration is lost.

Throw the dust sheets over the Cave of Making.
Pile the thirteen volumes of the dictionary
alphabetically upon the floor.
Archaism returns to the antiquary,
logodaedaly to the Admen and the Law.
The leaves are silent. These oracles are dumb,
and history all that mystery can become.

Send Caliban back to Roy Plomley.
Call Ariel down from the shrouds.
Storm and sweet airs dissolve together
as that man with the hanging look simply
vanishes into the crowd.
All that it could take the magic took.
His staff lies broken: undrowned, his book.

Rosehill

i.

Cumulus forms and drifts.

                    Some
part of the children who play
here is light chasing on
an empty playground.

          Their voices
as they rise have distance in.

        On the edge of
the moving city they look over
the houses their grandparents
called *mushroom growth*.

ii.

History fell behind us,
in a crook of the river,
on another, lower hill,

a groundwork that goes down ten
centuries, or seven feet.

Two miles west, on a gravel terrace,
our speech is as a strong city:

in three names three gates still stand,
though the Southgate has fallen

– our security that the names come
unbidden, from time out of mind.

Here weather is the change a
shadow makes in the shape of
a wall, and the hours a depth
in the colour of the stone,

a past that we commute to,
old centres only the banks
can afford.

Bus queues line the Cornmarket,
bound for the outer estates.

The fare stage is in Old French.

iii.

Pitched into fields, on hillsides
where the postwar tide left them,
before the next high water,

seven prefabs are still here
to recall our origins.

The hill's first settlement. We
walk to the shops at the Top.
We wait at the roundabout
where the bus turns.

Change become stationary.
Silence made to be broken.

iv.

There is no way to know us.

An ungenerous culture,
nothing of our life appears.

Over eighty thousand years
what changes?
The caves come outside the rock,

the housebacks terrace the hill
under the terraces of
travelling cloud.

There is no way to know us,
except as we know ourselves,

involuntarily,
in the silences the old

still call *an angel passing*,
in the skin tremor they say is

someone walking on my grave,

or in an *eye* we call *the mind's*
opening, in children looking down

to their homes foreshortened at their feet.

Cloud darkens. The rain moves in,
and the hill is lit windows,
riding lights.

         The streets below
are shoreline houses, still points
beside an estuary.

v.

Winter sunlight defines us,
momentary hill figures,
in negative on lit slopes:

we are a footstep's shadow;
we are the echo of light.

As you turn to me, and in
turning take my arm,

the sun travels through our coats
to form unwoven matter
on fibres of light

          and here
this slight and linear dark
where your shadow and mine cross.

Winter heat in the pavement;
a pigeon suns on a roof;

and for half or a minute
we are as old as the light.

The Broken Road

Water on the fields
sedged with white grass

Tarmac over flints
the flints wearing through

Walking again
along the broken road:

is it the road bears us up
or the brokenness?

As the upper sky darkens
a depth enters the pools,
corn gold suffuses the grass

The stones grow luminous as they dim

Out of the blue-blacks of the tar
the blues effloresce

Light is a bloom
a pollen of blue

It powders up under our feet

Culvert

Stone stepping over,
cushioning arch
of cut and canted
stones, road's instep
riding the dip

of older workings
with the grain of the rock,
weatherings underground,
where water tells
another story

at cross-purposes
to this: bright threads
under memory, that pool
in memory's loss. Here
is a Roman thread,

a forethought of stone.

Rites of Passage

*to Anthony Conran, in the year of his marriage,
the birth of his first child, and his father's death.*

Comfortable words, framed
in darker times than ours,
are ruined archways,

rusted gates, lych gate
or kissing gate, beaten paths
to love or death

that dwindle out of use.
As our forefathers knew,
their ways are grass

– a by-way their sense of
comfortable, a castle stump
in the marches

that marks where a language
lost its fight. The formless
is given ground.

A name thumbed from the map
wears a way back to
the capital.

Death blues a nail, and
climbs the ring finger
to the heart.

We are raided by
the inarticulate. *Be sober,
be vigilant,*

the Apostle says – watchwords since
requisitioned by General Booth
and Captain Lynch

while *our adversary . . .*
as a roaring lion is
all but extinct.

The last enemy is
amnesia. The synapses
lapse in the mind,

the keystones fall to the grass.
Roadmenders are few, roadmakers
almost none. All

but lost to philology
the adjective's active
ability

to say *comfort* where there is
nothing to be said, at *Brig o' Dread*
to find foothold.

Or before this other, this
excellent mystery, to give good luck
at the threshold.

The language is at a loss:
uncomfortable, unaccustomed
and unversed.

"Now cool it!" – honeyed voices
over the rasp of Jeremiah
grinding his axe –

"Adam has transplanted the Garden.
Time is becoming habitable
for the first time.

Ask the dead. They'd be here tomorrow
with *'We should have your problems!'* "
And so they would.

They'd have the transplanted Garden
in one perpetual season,
stationary

in an arrested prime: every
floret held back to a *floruit*,
a moment's grace

or else . . . the disgrace,
the fade, the dissolve into
incoherence.

What would they say, the stone-
breaking dead, who broke the unspoken
into metal,

links of an embanked and culverted
spine, a strait road that stretched
to meet their god?

Death is the way we live. In time
the myth comes, and gathers us
to our long home.

Only ours is comfortless:
the consuming young; obsolescence
built-into the old.

Can we match our forefathers' active
speech, that *made* a good marriage
or a good death,

from the passive registry
the language has become, the syllables'
expanding files

of *developmental life crises*
or *maladaptive conflict
situations*?

While the elderly subscribe
to *Death Education*, a course in
creative dying.

A feather print in the rock,
psychosis is all we keep
of the *psyche*,

the brush of a fossil wing.

Homage to James K. Baxter

Despair is the only gift;
When it is shared, it becomes a different thing.
James K. Baxter, from *Runes*
posthumously published by Oxford University Press in 1973

A newsagent taking in the first papers
would see us taking shape at the counter,
the ghost trade, come for Mars and Old Holborn, sugar and smoke.

Each morning, a shortchanging of the shadows,
as they rose from areas and stairwells,
sleepless from skinpopping methedrine.

Ah! the nights on the road
on a mattress, 'on the move' through
the bleak indoors. Joe Tex sang of

stogies as we rolled our Social Security
into straights, played *Indianapoly* through the small hours:
the speed kings, firing on half an amp.

And yet it was almost good, to be one
of a tacit company, to be men without women,
low lifeforms in a basement room.

Only a few of us became serious ghosts.
Our selves shadowed us. Only the present
can be lost in Lethe,

as I would lose it now, for your company.
But the light breaks. And already the shapes
are forming at the counter.

Waiting for the Day

Plimsoles takes the floor. Blossoms as the Bar
whoops and whistles. As if he were
treading water, as if rough music were the water
where a strange nature uncurls and flowers,
he slow-motions to the door. Already in replay,
an old clip run and re-run, his white hipsters
step and flare. His white raincoat
capes and swirls. He is all woman.
We are all eyes.

Sullen, in black, his fetch
steps tersely at his side.

Shanghai? Marseilles? Tilbury.
Last light over warehouse roofs.
Darkness asphalts the waste ground.

Not a sound when he re-enters.
Buys an armful of beer cans. Outside,
hurls them one by one against the wall,

repeatedly. Gathers them up, shoulders
hunched in the white T-shirt.
Cradles them back to the ship.

We nurse our halves. Tomorrow
if a crew is short – someone
fails to report – one of us
will get a ship. On completion
of the trip, union papers.

Buzzards

Hook beak, hawk wings and cross-hatchings
are old service patches

on battledressed veterans, who pudder
on their allotments of air.

Except the insignia will not fade.
Only the old soldiery never dies.

They have only to lift over the skyline
and the rook flak rises.

Each morning their mobbed shapes come
mewing from the wood, silhouettes of

a fear without armistice,
feather of a bad dream.

All afternoon they crest the telegraph poles,
the Third Reich in moult,

waiting for the earthworms to emerge,
waiting for the roads to deliver their dead.

In Transit

i. The Young Soldiers

Two weeks each of them has been away from home,
having a man made of him. In the legend
of small brothers. Behind reminiscence
in the Public Bar. And two days a figure
home on leave. Arms linked, the girls in the Disco
cross the floor in threes: hello, they say, stranger.

Strange to be anyone, invisibility
at the back of the class retained them so long.
Strange as their exchange of nowhere for nowhere,
out of work on the streets of Bolton and Colne
or well-paid patrolling the streets of Belfast.
They talk vaguely of a tour in Germany.

They think over and over of coming out
with a trade. The train removes them south once more
for combat training. Now they are drinking like
troopers; and it could be because they're half-cut
they're telling you this, their hands shake and they are
crying. In the same breath keeled over asleep.

ii. The Weapons Instructor

And even the experience he did not choose
is of no use.
                    In his mind as the train moves north
the hare's scream the boy gave as he jigged and shuddered,
cramped over the trigger.
                              'The Powers That Be, in their
wisdom...': an officer's way of saying he was refused
an engineering course, ten years ago. Since when
he has served the Powers in their wisdom,
sergeant to the raw generations, technical
specialist into an old sweat of thirty three.

'Well, keep an eye on him, Sergeant.' As if
he hadn't. As if he had spoken out of turn.

Course continues. He continues to keep an eye.
Course ends with the new rifle, for use in Ulster.
Which all the recruits always take seriously.
Which this one takes in rigid hands.
                              And at once fires,
a spasm of rapid fire in which he reels and screams,
still firing.
                    One man killed. Two of them all their strength
to get the gun off him/release him from the gun.

Manslaughter. And the hare's scream of the slaughterer.
A hare's brain of fear.
                    Put it all down to
experience. Wisdom is for the officers.

iii. The Professionals

Stout McGuinness and *Twomey's Flit* fill the carriage,
cassettes of jigs and reels, recorded off-duty
in pubs, in front rooms after hours – and over here
not quite the thing, as glances from the businessmen
imply. Have they gone native? The usual Yahoos.

Such is emergency, this side of the water.
A motley of khakis, camouflage and civvies,
a shambles of boots and shoes: soldiers returning
in the privilege of action, all-licensed by
sheer relief; who none the less turn down their cassettes,

being, more than anything, tired. And settle themselves.
Close down. The hours are absorbed into their posture,
one with the hours of the nights of their tour, the days
of years they have traded in for a trade, a skilled
future. Lloyds would not insure their education:

but the roster will see them back over the water,
from exercises off Cyprus with the Sixth Fleet,
manoeuvres on Aldershot or Luneberg Heath,
to the narrow, boarded streets where they have become
more or less at home among those who resent them.

The Doppel Gang
or Better By Half, wherein the Hasidic Principle is applied to History.

Others, to restore the balance, claim that . . . there were actually two Baal Shem Tovs and that the Hasidic movement was founded . . . by the other.
Elie Wiesel: *Souls on Fire*

His sonatas will end up as curl papers; his landlady use his symphony for lining a trunk; several execrable Irish ballads live on. As a violinist he barely, as they say, scrapes a living. Of late, the further to fiddle his creditors, has followed the Armies to Brussels, where he has earned the sobriquet of *Maréchal Nez*. There was a time his looks brought him heirs and disgraces. Now the wits ask if he bows with his nose. The *Beau Monde* is thick with wits. No matter. Five francs are not to be sneezed at. Another set forms up on the floor. He shakes himself: "Stop woolgatherin', Wellesley." Up strikes the music. And there he is again, a stooped, unmilitary shadow, second fiddle at the Duchess of Richmond's Ball, on the eve of Waterloo.

Litter blows over the Park. The length and breadth of the Crystal Palace, the sunlight exhibits the dust. Hobnails grind between the aisles. Knuckles rap, sizing up the wood of the stands. Hereon had men glimpsed a City. The New Jerusalem, with working models. With the last word in Progress, the Alpha and Omega: universal suffrage and sewerage. But here comes the universal appliance, a man in his five wits. Why, it's Albert Francis Charles Augustus Emanuel. And looking quite the everyday article, in moleskin trousers, flannel shirt and a stud. Not, it seems, the gentleman from Saxe-Coburg-Gotha. But from the German colony in Manchester. Demolition contractor to the Great Exhibition. He shoulders a length of heart of oak. "Long as there's one to set it up," he winks, "t'other'll clear it away."

Outside, the sirocco. Inside, as cool as a catamite's fingertip. The houseboys, the Arab, the Italian, and the Swede, are deep in Monopoly. Foundation Studies. They plan to be sleek and sixty, rich gourmands of little delicacies. Like *milord*, who has just switched off the wireless. Really, if it wasn't that it so worried the Vichy, he would throw the thing away. All that guff *On The Beaches*. That antiphonal fuss over *The Few*. And now, believe it or not, *Their Finest Hour*. That the language should be so harrowed! Spencer is quite disgusted with Winston. He dispatches a winged word: "You know, duckie, I sometimes wonder which of us is camp."

The Hooded Gods

*three male gods of healing, fertility, and the underworld,
from a stone plaque in Housesteads Museum, Hadrian's Wall.*

These are the odds and sods among the gods,
the other ranks, the omnipresences,
teamen, charmen, male midwives: the daily helps
from history's basement, the caretakers

who rarely come to light. They have become
their deliverances, their many hands
beneath notice and now beyond telling.
They surface from the sleep of history

whose care suffuses history like sleep,
powers of recovery and repair
who keep the middle watch, the graveyard shift,
the seamsters who knit up the ravelled sleeve.

Empire succeeds empire over their heads.
The paces centuries set in the Wall
have doubled under artillery wheels.
Now low-flying Phantoms ghost from the stones.

Their histories are the interleaves,
the pages happiness has written white.
They show as lapses in the chronicle,
or specks of dialect in letters home.

No stars in their eyes. No shrinking either.
These are the hard core. These are the heart's wood.
Three grey bottles still standing on the Wall.
Three pollards who can make a fist of green.

Freebooter

Carrying a timber twice his height
along the verge of the A43,

shoulder freight
coasting beside the tonnage of lorries,

he balances a few jars
against the ache in his collar bone,

bringing a windfall to land.

Anonymous and sharp
in his flat cap and mac,

the original fly one,

good luck comes of him,
the bright intervals

at his heels.

Rain is steaming off the roads

as he makes up channel
on a cushy number,

a quid
within walking distance,

time on his shoulder.

Smoke Without Fire

Where only the single leaf
of the tide turns,
a bonfire's breath

forms in the air,
in the ascension of
three flakes of ash

as they revolve and
sink, are re-assumed
and relapse. Sun

on the salt grass
releases blue heat
in a thermal

where three buzzards clamber
and slide. They ship one
wing, feint at another

climbing as they
side-slip down, then
soar to stoop again,

a deciduous movement
over greywacke-shale,
on a breath of a tree-

less cliff, where ash
floats through woodsmoke
a wing's breadth in from the sea.

The Night Self

Fin nos, wrth fwrw lludded.

Now the puckish humours leave your face.
The skin acknowledges the bone.
The presence is as one
of the individual and the race.
In motherhood you will not look so strong,
nor in death so young.

Lower Lumb Mill

For Ellie; and for the teachers and pupils of Nicholls Ardwick
School, Manchester, who spent a week writing at Lumb Bank.

i.

Here are the reins of
the work horse, the traces
of water in harness,

still handstitched in stone:
and not slack, though water
falls in idleness, though weather

buffs and beeches the black
of the chimney that once blackened
the beeches; and still rises

out of all proportion
to rocks and stones and trees,
a first draught, a delineation

of valleys since transfigured
by cubes and planes and cones,
a shadow of Hell or Halifax,

of mills and manufactories
wherever water ran,
terracings and resurfacings

worn through again as the work
moves away. Now tree shadows
box the walls. Green thoughts

wash at the drystone. Or,
under the petrodollar's
green shade, green thoughts

walk down from Lumb Bank. Between
anorak and wellingtons, jay's
wingflashes of tight sateen

as the walking disco, Angela,
Jennifer, Beverley and Mo,
sends a green blue beat through

the thoughtful thrush-tap on stone
of the geologist's hammer
Mohammed would like to have,

and stirs Farah's tree of silence,
just broken into the first leaf
of her sketchbook. Our other lives

star the valley, the Persephone
in each of us given five days
above ground. Half-thoughts, slim chances,

huddle at the valley's rim,
wind-silvered underleaves,
the ghosts of our fits and starts.

'Where to go from here?'
A rainflash of fieldfares turns
into dust shaken from a duster.

Out of memory a ring-dove calls,
Darby, be true, Darby . . .
And truly, where can we go?

ii.

Even as we ask, a road
finds our feet. Gently down,
under moss'd tree roots,

between banks of primroses.
Sunlight mullioned through branches.
Madrigals of blackbird and thrush.

Now the hill is a honeycomb
of lanes we wander two by two,
in conspiracies of reverence,

little arches of whispering heads.
Each couple through its kissing gate
threads onto a village green

the generations in their loveknots
have stitched as white as the may.
Here is a month of Sundays.

Afternoon is a tune
from Elgar, on which the sun,
in a setting by Vaughan-Williams,

never sets. Elms constable
the high clouds. Yews cloister
the path. Lawns are palladian

with light and dark. We walk
under great protections,
into wise enclosures.

Distantly, distinctly,
as clear as the voice of Clare,
a yellowhammer sings,

*A little bit of bread
and no cheese. A little bit
of bread and no cheese.*

46

The lawns spin like roulette wheels.
Cloud smokes in a ring. Towers of
coin rise on fields of baize.

The Trade Winds blow us back
to our places. Beverley? Mo?
Unheard of. Battened under hatches

Bristol fashion. Ship's ballast
to the Indies, or King
Cotton's fields. Mohammed?

Locked in a Kipling ballad
– one of many who move
between the lines, and serve

the twenty six soldiers
of lead, appearing only
as points of silence.

As for me, who should I be
but Hodge? The original blot
on the landscape, the labourer

beyond the ha-ha, who trespasses
twice a year on the park
of English poetry, the blackface

morrising and mumming
through the gates. Clodhopper.
Clown. Brother to the ox.

iii.

Now *Teacher! Teacher!* pages me
through the wood. Wordsworth sermons
in stones. Tennyson riffles

in the brook. Those two metallic
tones pulse. Siren song. Nerve
twitch. Quartz chimes on my wrist.

Hard to learn my own lesson:
to listen as voices rise
on other paths, to look up

into the star haze of buds
and see the twigs jigsaw
and piece the light. One step

up the slope, at eye level,
a beech sapling breaks
into a galaxy. Two arcs

swirl out, encircling
a space the buds orbit
in planetary calm.

How they keep station and
constellation, equidistant
in the wind-flattened flame!

Last night, all at sea
in the surge of the bluebeat,
a white face in the trough

of a wave, I trod water
and watched you drown
one step away. Then someone

took a hand. We circled
and centred in a star.
The star flowered and flowed

back into bud, we swung out
and danced in, our hands linked
and rising to a crest,

rising to gull shrieks and skirls,
triumph and delight and hope and fear,
one wave of the earth.

This morning was full tide,
a mirror of quiet. We were deep
in our reflections. We mused

into coffee mugs. Toasted marshmallows
on the fire. The hearth held us
in its gravity. I watched you

as you sat in the sofa corner
listening to Sue. Listening
is your trance. I shall always see you

poised over the ashtray
on your knee. You lean back
on your elbow to inhale,

you lift your face. Eyes closed,
you dream a moment, Delphic
in the haze. This morning

was different. You leaned forward,
listening head and shoulders
to Sue. Whose life was it?

Who was listening in you?
You were rigid with recall.
I glimpsed you at fifteen,

the family manager:
your father in and out of work,
a man of hopeless charm,

your mother in the damp flat,
bright-eyed on barbiturates;
and you the ghost of a child

grown-up half-grown, mothering
and motherless. How we are hurt
into being! Made and marred

in the same breath. To watch you
kindling in a smile, immediate,
healing, acute, is to watch you

give yourself away.

iv.

And so I come
to the valley's head, where the path
turns towards home. *Come out!*

Come out! sweetly reasons
a song thrush, *Over the moor*
lies The New Delight. And I think

of all the streets we have paced,
all our unseeing circuits
of the park. Each despair.

Each renewal. Of whole families
who war in us. Each mother
and father of a row. "Stop being

so bloody English!" you once shot
at my verray parfit gentil knyght.
And down I came off my high horse.

My love, how would you disarm us now?
Of our hurts? Our history?
Unhappiness is a ghetto

– we turn in blind alleys
where words have their own quarrels
and a touch ends in a shrug.

If I could catch what is baffled
and battles in us, negotiates
and is unnegotiable...

I think of Jennifer, farmed out
to her grandmother in Barbados,
bringing home all she has to bring:

her difference, her awkward truth.
And then of Sue, meeting her mother
outside the cinema once a week.

They buy their popcorn and hardly speak.
It's early days. But as the lights dim
they sit together. Their faces lift.

They are looking out of next Friday
in Ardwick. Mo bites her lip
on the check-out, her eyes down

under the queue of eyes: "they watch
as each item is put through: they know
your mistakes even before you do."

While in the corner shop, tin
by tin, Mohammed takes stock
of his mother's English. Then sighs

and begins again. Concentrations
of work and love, mirrored
in the plate glass of the malls,

multiplied in the windows
of the estates; and still locked
into this valley's stone setts

and revetments, the work surface
that is all we inherit
of the earth: the wheel-shaft

deep as a canal lock; the dye-pits
that square-off these upper slopes;
the waggon-road's steady gradient

my feet already incline to
as second nature. *Come out!*
Come out! insists the song thrush

and a wind shivers the ferns
on the bank. Remember how
as lovers we moved from sign

to sign? How two magpies glided
the length of our path? Goldfinches
glinted from hedge to hedge

braiding our walk? Every day
brought its confirmation,
its laying-on of wings.

Now I watch the full moon
of your forehead – *swan's breast*,
the bards would have sung, *blossom*

of the heaven bough – cloud over
and your shoulders "conform
to the yoke", you once wrote,

a slight, preoccupied stoop,
and my arms reach out in tenderness,
blind tenderness, to hold you

and renew the harm. At this point
there is no sign. Only the road's
grits and micas, the scuffed shine

that could prove another circuit
of hell, or the last mile
we must go, though it strip us

to the bare bone.

Skara Brae

for Frances and Adam

The dunes of peat ash,
the skears of scraped-out shells,
the gravel of animal bones, the flocks of sand,

all worked to a hard mothering,
a weathertight skin of clay
hummocked over the huts: embryos

in chamber tombs, mound dwellers
under their own midden, they pressed
out of the vortex engraved on their pots,

childbearing children, dead at twenty;
learned to bait bone splinters with limpets
softened in freshwater; to twist heather

into simmons tethering the stock; to staunch bleeding
with the puff-ball's black gauze; step by step
moved away from the swallow-hole.

In fine weather they broke surface. Knappings
and food scraps littered the roof of the mound.
Here are the good days, the hours in the sun.

Water rose as they bent to the spring,
the ram's horn of water rose for them,
and they saw themselves as water's face,

as luck's two hands, fastening sheepskin
with a bone pin, polishing oxhide
with an ox knuckle. They scoured

Note: Skara Brae is a Stone Age village in the sand dunes of Orkney
covered over by a great storm in prehistoric times and uncovered by
another storm in the last century. 'Skear' is northern dialect for a mussel
scar, an off-shore ridge or sandbank exposed at low tide.

the sea's scourings: soft horns of driftwood
that were American spruce; dry foam of pumice
from Icelandic lava flows. Worked on their luck,

grinding a gannet's bone into the pumice
until it was sharp enough for an awl,
hollowing an antler until it held an axehead.

Bored through cattle teeth. Bored through a walrus tusk.
Out of salvage and scrap built up a bead hoard,
a string of good days. Began to bank on their luck.

Set spy-holes into passages valved with stone slabs,
secreted it in treasure cells. Until the mound was
another mouth on the foreshore, swallowing all it could use.

Hunger is stilled now. Now there is only stillness:
the hearth swept; the quernstone at rest in the quern,
in the churn-hole of rock, a fossil of water in spate.

Here is the life they hardly knew, the quiet enshrined
on the shelves of their stone dresser, or glimpsed
out to sea, the horizon's back shelf of light

still clear and still out of reach: a persistence
of charms and undergleams, of secrecies and stowings,
a necklace tucked into the heather of the boxbed

or spilled over the threshold. White dribbles down,
the gutted fish leaking its roe, the skinned hare
her milk under the skin. All their luck let slip

at the last, the string snapped on the narrow door
they scrambled through, as the wind darkened
and the dunes began to run like the sea.

At Vanishing Point

para Eugenia en El Cántaro

This morning we talk again
under the bony plum,

whose fruit, like a stone
sucked in the mouth,

can outwit thirst. I sit
on the garden seat as on

the bench of the ship of souls,
lashed to my oar. Almost hear,

between the tick-birds and
the parakeets, a gull's keen,

invoking solitude, the doom
of the Seafarer, who dreams

of a hearth and companions, and wakes
to the ice of the whale-road.

My salve for hard times
is to make them harder still.

You do that too. You will
when I leave. Lock yourself

in your painter's attic
in Bogotá. Work to

the wry songs of Bola de Nieve.
Geni, you and I are two

of a kind. I find you
on the bench beside me.

Above us, like a daydream, like a thought
moored between two pillars of cloud,

El Cántaro, the house you built
out of stubbornness, out of shipwreck.

It is just pencilled in
against the sky. Just held

at the point of erasure.
Built of shadings, cross-hatchings,

a pencil sharpening the whiteness
of paper, constructing

a moebius strip of light,
endless galleries, rising

scales of roof, ascending
and descending stairs.

The pencil sketched, suffered
erasure, sketched again.

One by one the variants
emerged. Plumped onto the page

and sank without trace. Stepped out
on their spindleshanks

and crumpled into the pits
of erasure, the hubbub of forms

jostling for life. Then the pencil
took wing. Took from the swift's wing

the long, honed line, that austere
primary glide. Took from the owl's wing

the crossing of tenons, that secondary
softness of flight. Something lifted

that could fly. Now we live under its wing.
Watch the diamond lattice compose the light

and the stairs rise in counterpoint. Hear
the three-part harmony in the turn of the stair.

Geni, we came here already erased.
All that life we lived on paper,

all the ways and means we had sketched
in our letters. What precise negations,

what scar-white lines your ghost must have crossed
to find me. I was a blankness walking

on the white fires of that grid.
Now we talk. My fingers touch the blade

of your shoulder. And are fingers
on warm skin. We touch as only survivors

can touch. Butterflies like blue water
lap the air. The charcoal tree has blossomed

into featherdusters of flame. We could walk down
to the Sumapaz, the Peaceable River,

naming the white humped cattle, the hawk
who is a call, a circling

shadowed by her young, the lizards
who are known only by their vanishing.

The Roof Tree

for Bibiana in Ladywell

Coming to call you for supper,
I enter a visible hush,
the cat's cradle of reflections
your writing lamp throws on the wall.
No more than glances off whitewash,
three or four spills of light, it seems
to open a luminous depth
of projections and precisions.
One triangle slants its clear field
across another's ridge of light,
as if the stars were focused there,
their constancies, their still waters
crystallised in a quartz of light.

A hand's breadth of transparency,
it forms above your head, one of
the stations I make in passing,
a scallop shell of quiet – and
would vanish if I came closer,
a silence in your own language
that is sounding the dry water
of these stones. I pause in the door,
afraid to break the first hair's breadths
of belonging, threads and sensings
that are making of this spare room
a familiar solitude,
a separateness that is home.

Downstairs your sister sits cross-legged
in the stereo's cockpit glow,
her body earthed and her headphones
filtering the empyrean
as a baroque trumpet ascends
through the firmament, its pinpoint
of angels feathering the blue.
While your mother sips her whisky
in front of a makeshift easel
– the stepladder with two nails in –
and contemplates these zinc yellows,
fragile, underwater yellows
whose phosphorus burns in water.

My notebook is open: but for once
it's enough to be house and home,
to set bowls on the low table
and wait. The stillness still holds you,
each separate stillness that shelves
beneath the archipelago
of lights. The house rides on silence.
And though the evening ahead
has an old magic, renewing
our ring of faces in firelight,
I would rather keep the quiet
of the lamps in their far reaches,
the depth of stars under the roof.

The clovers in the salt-glazed jar
– one find in another's keeping –
raise their hussar heads and brisk out
their purple shakos. And I steel
every nerve for your going.
Intimate and homely, like breaths
drawn in sleep, the silences stir
and sigh. Catches and quickenings.
Easings and settlings. A massive,
multitudinous calm, as though
the roof tree had branched and blossomed,
a chestnut setting a candle
in every window of leaf.